GOD'S ANGELS
Messengers on a Mission

Angela M. Burrin

Illustrated By Maria Cristina Lo Cascio

Dear Reader, This is a book about angels!

Before you turn the page, let me tell you some fun facts about angels. Even before God created the earth, he created the angels—thousands upon thousands and ten thousand upon ten thousand of them. That's a lot of angels! Angels are spirits, so they will never die. Angels are more perfect and glorious than any creatures on earth.

A special privilege the angels have is that they actually see God. Day and night they never stop singing, "Holy, holy, holy is the Lord God Almighty, who was and is and who is to come!" (Revelation 4:8). Angels also go between heaven and earth. Imagine the ladder that Jacob dreamed about reaching all the way to heaven, with angels climbing up and down it! (Genesis 28:12).

Angels are God's servants and messengers. In fact, the word "angel" means messenger. In this book you will read stories of how angels had some very important assignments. And their number-one assignment was to carry out God's loving plan to have his sons and daughters with him forever and ever. That includes you! The good news is that angels are still on assignment. That's why you have your very own guardian angel!

5

6

Chapter One
An Angel with a Fiery Sword

(Genesis 3)

God always wanted to share his love with others. So God created the first man and woman, Adam and Eve. He gave them a beautiful place to live called the Garden of Eden. He let them name all the animals. God's angels watched all of this happen.

God wanted Adam and Eve to live there with him forever. There was only one very important rule. He said, "Because I love you, do not eat the fruit of the tree of the knowledge of good and evil. It will hurt our friendship."

Satan knew about this rule. He tempted Adam and Eve, saying, "If you eat the fruit of the tree of the knowledge of good and evil, you will be like God." They disobeyed their heavenly Father and chose to eat the forbidden fruit.

Although Adam and Eve had sinned, their Father still loved them. But they had to leave the Garden of Eden. God placed an angel holding a fiery sword at the entrance to the garden so they could not enter again. Oh no! What was God going to do now?

Chapter Two
The Angel Gabriel

(Luke 1:15-25; 57-80)

Nothing is impossible for God. He came up with an amazing plan: he would send his Son, Jesus, to earth to save people from their sins. Then they could live with him forever.

For thousands of years, God prepared the way for Jesus to come. Finally, it was time. God sent one of his highest-ranking angels—the Archangel Gabriel—to a priest called Zechariah.

Gabriel said, "Zechariah, don't be afraid. God has heard your prayer for a baby. Your wife, Elizabeth, will have a son. You must name him John. He will be filled with the Holy Spirit. John will tell the people to repent and prepare their hearts for the coming of my Son."

Zechariah said, "But Elizabeth and I are too old to have children." The angel replied, "I am Gabriel. I've come straight from being in God's presence. Because you doubted, you will not be able to speak until your son is born."

Nine months later, Elizabeth had a baby. She wanted to call him John. Zechariah wrote, "His name is John." Then Zechariah was able to speak. He sang, "God, you are faithful. You never forget us. My son, John, is part of your great saving plan!"

9

Chapter Three
Another Important Message

(Luke 1:26-56; Matthew 1:18-25)

God said to Gabriel, "Now I have another important assignment for you. I want you to give a message to a very special woman named Mary, who lives in Nazareth."

When Gabriel appeared to her, Mary was frightened. But he said, "Greetings, Mary! Don't be afraid. Your heavenly Father is pleased with you. You are to give birth to a son, and you are to name him Jesus. He will be great, and of his kingdom there will be no end."

"How will this happen?" Mary asked him. Gabriel said, "The Holy Spirit will come upon you, and the baby who will be born will be called holy, the Son of the Most high. You will call him Jesus."

Mary's heart was full of joy. And because she always wanted to please God, she said, "I am the Lord's servant. Yes! Let it happen as you say." Then Gabriel returned to heaven.

When Mary's future husband, Joseph, learned that she was expecting a child, he was worried. But God comforted Joseph by sending an angel to him in a dream. The angel said, "Joseph, don't be afraid to take Mary as your wife. It is through the Holy Spirit that Mary has conceived this child. He will be the Savior of the world."

Chapter Four
Angels Tell Shepherds about Jesus' Birth

(LUKE 2:1-20)

Now it was time for the angels to announce the birth of Jesus!

Mary and Joseph had to travel to Bethlehem to register in a census. But there were so many people there that they couldn't find a place to spend the night. Finally, an innkeeper let them stay in his stable.

That very night Jesus was born. Mary wrapped Jesus in swaddling cloths and laid him on straw in the animals' feeding manger. The ox and the donkey breathed on Jesus to keep him warm.

Some shepherds were in a field, keeping watch over their flock at night. An angel appeared to them, surrounded by a bright light. The shepherds were very frightened, but the angel said, "Don't be afraid. I have good news! Here in this town of Bethlehem, the Messiah has been born. You will find him in a stable lying in a manger."

Suddenly, the angel was joined by thousands of other angels! They started singing, "Glory to God in the highest, and on earth peace to those on whom his favor rests."

The shepherds were so excited. They rushed down the hillside and found Jesus in the stable with Mary and Joseph. When they returned to the fields, they were singing God's praises.

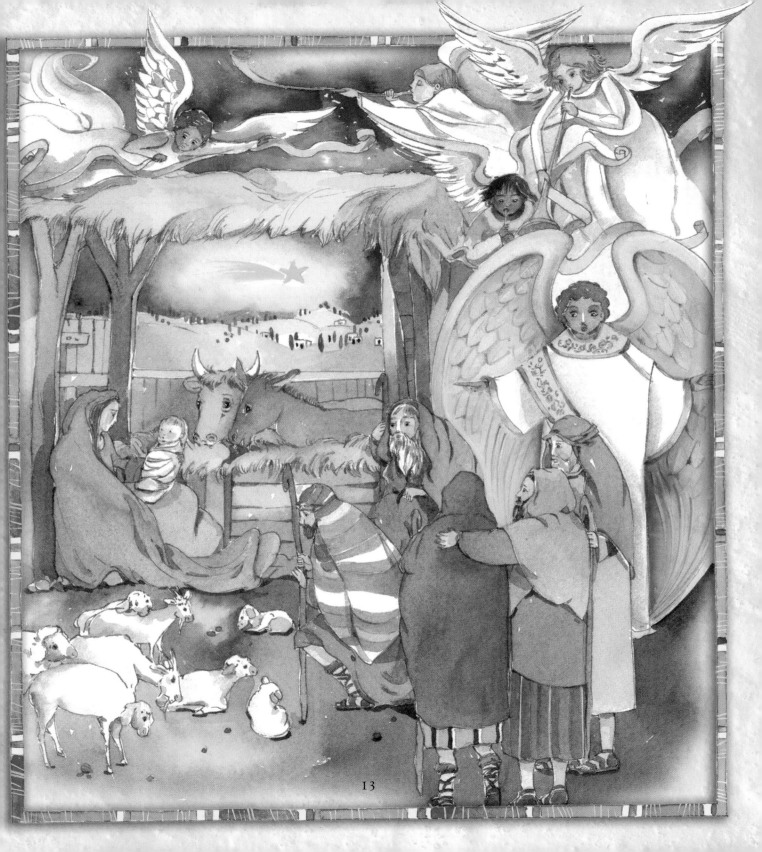

Chapter Five
An Angel Warns Joseph in a Dream

(MATTHEW 2)

God is always in control. He had a perfect plan for Jesus' life. No one could make it go wrong. But someone did try. His name was King Herod.

After Jesus was born, three magi from the East arrived in Jerusalem, asking, "Where is the newborn king of the Jews? We saw his star." Herod was very worried. He didn't want Jesus to take his place as king. Instead, he wanted him killed.

The magi found Jesus in Bethlehem and offered him gifts of gold, frankincense, and myrrh. Then an angel appeared to Joseph in a dream. "Hurry, take Jesus and Mary, his mother, and go to Egypt," the angel said. "Stay there until I tell you. Herod wants to kill Jesus." Joseph woke up and told Mary about his dream. They quickly planned their escape to Egypt. It was a long journey. Mary sat on a donkey holding Jesus, and Joseph walked alongside.

After King Herod died, Joseph saw another angel in a dream. The angel said, "It is now safe to go back to the land of Israel." Joseph and Mary were so excited to go back home!

Chapter Six
Angels Comfort Jesus

(Matthew 4:1-11)

Jesus loved his heavenly Father. He was always praying and listening to him. When he was thirty years old, he knew it was time for him to take the next step in his Father's amazing plan. So after being baptized in the Jordan River, he went into the desert. There he prayed and fasted for forty days and forty nights.

During this time, Satan tempted Jesus three times. Satan knew Jesus was hungry, so he said, "Command these stones to be turned into bread." Jesus said, "No! My Father will provide all that I need."

Next, Satan took Jesus to the top of the temple in Jerusalem and said, "If you are God, jump down and God's angels will take care of you." Jesus said, "No! I won't put God to the test." After these three temptations, Satan left him.

Finally, Satan took him to the top of a high mountain and said, "I'll give you all these kingdoms if you will worship me." Jesus said, "No! I will worship and serve only God."

Jesus' Father saw everything. Once again he called on his angels. "I'm sending you to Jesus in the desert," God said. "He's exhausted, lonely, hungry, and thirsty. Comfort my Son and take care of him for me." What do you think the angels did for Jesus?

Chapter Seven
An Angel in the Garden of Gethsemane

(LUKE 22:39-46)

For three years Jesus taught the crowds and healed the sick. "My Father loves you," he said. "He wants to free you from sin so you can you can be his friend forever." But now came the saddest part of God's saving plan—the death of Jesus.

Jesus ate his last supper with his disciples. He took bread and wine and changed them into his body and blood. He said, "Do this in memory of me."

Then he said to his disciples, "Come with me to the Garden of Gethsemane." When they arrived, Jesus said, "My friends, sit here while I go and pray."

Jesus went off by himself. He wanted time alone with his Father. Jesus prayed, "Father, take this cup from me, but not my will but yours be done." He prayed these words three times. He was so upset that he sweated drops of blood.

Every time he went back to his disciples, he found them sleeping. But God the Father saw the suffering of his son. He called one of his angels, and immediately the angel was at Jesus' side to comfort him.

The soldiers came and arrested Jesus. He didn't argue or complain. He loved everyone so much that he was willing to suffer for them.

Chapter Eight
Angels Announce That Jesus Is Alive!

(LUKE 24:1-12)

On Good Friday, Jesus was crucified. Jesus' mother Mary, his disciple John, Mary Magdalene, and some other women stood at the foot of his cross. For three hours, the sky was dark. Then Jesus said, "It is finished." He bowed his head and died.

Joseph of Arimathea, a secret friend of Jesus, wrapped Jesus' body in a clean cloth and carried it to a tomb. Then he rolled a large stone across the entrance to the tomb.

Early in the morning on the third day—Easter Sunday—some women went to the tomb. To their surprise, the stone had been rolled away. They went in, but they didn't find the body of Jesus.

While all this was happening, there was great excitement in heaven. "It is time for you to announce that Jesus has risen from the dead," God told two of his angels.

Then the women saw the angels wearing dazzling white robes. They were very frightened, but the angels said, "Don't be afraid. Jesus is not here. He has risen from the dead, just as he said he would. Come and see the place where he lay."

The women were overjoyed. They ran to tell the disciples the wonderful news: Jesus had risen from the dead!

Chapter Nine
An Angel Helps Peter Escape

(Acts 12)

The news of Jesus' resurrection spread quickly. Many people came to believe in him. But King Herod wasn't happy. He killed James, one of Jesus' disciples. Then he put Peter is prison. "There is only one thing we can do," said Peter's friends. "We must pray and ask God to save him."

God heard their prayers. Once again he called upon one of his angels, saying, "I'm sending you to rescue Peter."

On the night before his trial, Peter was sleeping between two soldiers. His wrists were tied up with two chains. Outside his cell there were two other guards. Suddenly, the cell was filled with light and God's angel stood by Peter. The angel tapped Peter to wake him up, saying, "Get up quickly!" The chains dropped from his wrists.

The angel then said, "Put on your belt, your shoes, your cloak, and follow me." Peter thought he was dreaming! They walked past the first guard and then the second. When they came to the locked iron gate leading out to the city, it opened by itself.

Outside of the prison, the angel led Peter down an alley and then suddenly disappeared. Peter finally realized he wasn't dreaming. He said to himself, "Now I know that God sent his angel to rescue me!

Chapter Ten
An Angel Tells Philip Where to Go

(ACTS 8:26-40)

Christians were getting into trouble for believing in Jesus. So some of them left Jerusalem and went to different cities and countries. One man, Philip, went to the city of Samaria. There he taught and healed people in the name of Jesus.

One day an angel appeared to Philip and said, "Go south on the desert road." So Philip started off.

On the road he heard a chariot coming. In it was an important person in charge of money for the queen of Ethiopia. The Holy Spirit said, "Go to that chariot." The Ethiopian man was reading the words of the prophet Isaiah. Philip asked, "Do you understand what you are reading?" The Ethiopian answered, "How can I unless someone explains it to me? Tell me, is the prophet Isaiah talking about himself or someone else?"

Philip got into the chariot, saying, "I will tell you everything about Jesus." When they saw some water, the Ethiopian asked Philip, "Will you baptize me in the name of Jesus? Together they went into the water.

After coming out of the water, the Holy Spirit suddenly took Philip away. The Ethiopian never saw him again. But because Philip had obeyed the angel, the Ethiopian received new life!

Guardian Angels . . . and More

God is always thinking about you. Because he loves you and wants you to be protected, he has chosen one of his angels to be your guardian angel. That's an incredible gift from God.

Although you can't see your guardian angel, he's always with you. His assignment is to help you and keep you safe on your journey to heaven. So your guardian angel really likes when you ask for his help. There is even a special prayer you can say to your guardian angel. And there is also a feast day for celebrating all the guardian angels—October 2. Wouldn't it be fun to have an "angel party" with some of your friends on that day?

St. Michael the Archangel is another angel you can pray to for help. He is known as the prince of the heavenly host. This powerful angel fought Lucifer and the other angels who chose not to obey God. Michael defeated them and sent them out of heaven. He will help you when you are tempted. The feast day of the Archangels Michael, Gabriel, and Raphael is on September 29.

Aren't angels awesome? Their last assignment will be to accompany Jesus when he returns in all his glory to earth. Wow, won't that be a wonderful day?

Thank you, God, for your angels!

Prayer to St. Michael the Archangel

St. Michael the Archangel, defend us in battle.
Be our defense against the wickedness and snares of the devil.
May God rebuke him, we humbly pray, and do thou,
O Prince of the heavenly hosts, by the power of God,
cast into hell Satan, and all the evil spirits
who prowl about the world seeking the ruin of souls. Amen.

Psalm 91:11-12

He has put his angels in charge of you.
They will watch over you wherever you go.
They will catch you with their hands.
And you will not hit your foot on a rock.

A Prayer to My Guardian Angel

Angel of God, my guardian dear,
To whom God's love commits me here,
Every day be at my side,
To light and guard,
To rule and guide. Amen.

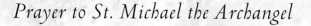

Dear Parents,

It has been such a joy writing this book about angels. I've especially loved sharing with your child how God involved his angels in bringing about his incredible plan of salvation. "For God so loved the world that he gave his only Son, so that everyone who believes in him might not perish but might have eternal life" (John 3:16).

Yes! Our heavenly Father longs for all of us—through Jesus—to be brought back into friendship with him and to experience eternal life. My prayer is for all children to know this truth and experience God's love from their earliest years.

There are many other stories about angels that I wasn't able to include here. I hope you will be able to read them with your child. I encourage you to continue the theme of God continually using his angels as instruments of his saving plan. You might also like to encourage your children to draw pictures of their own angel stories!

May all who read this book be greatly blessed!

Angela M. Burrin

Published in 2018 in the U.S. and Canada by
The Word Among Us Press
7115 Guilford Road, Suite 100
Frederick, MD 21704

ISBN: 978-1-59325-342-4

Publishing Director: Annette Reynolds
Art Director: Gerald Rogers
Pre-production: Doug Hewitt

Printed and bound in Malaysia
September 2018